W9-AUU-885

TRAVEL WITH THE GREAT EXPLORERS

Explore with
Hernando de Soto

Rachel Stuckey

Crabtree Publishing Company
www.crabtreebooks.com

Crabtree Publishing Company
www.crabtreebooks.com

Author: Rachel Stuckey

Managing Editor: Tim Cooke

Designer: Lynne Lennon

Picture Manager: Sophie Mortimer

Design Manager: Keith Davis

Editorial Director: Lindsey Lowe

Children's Publisher: Anne O'Daly

Crabtree Editorial Director: Kathy Middleton

Crabtree Editor: Petrice Custance

Proofreader: Wendy Scavuzzo

**Production coordinator
and prepress technician:** Tammy McGarr

Print coordinator: Katherine Berti

Written and produced for Crabtree Publishing Company
by Brown Bear Books

Photographs:

Front Cover: Alamy: Prisma Archivo l; **NM History Museum:** Kate Nelson br; **Shutterstock:** Photo Image cr, Steven Russell Smith Photos tr.

Interior: Alamy: Classic Image 11bc, Grainger NYC 10b, North Wind Picture Archives 10t, 15t, 17b, 18bl, 19, 29t, 29b, Prisma Archivo 5bl, 24-25; courtesy **Architect of the Capitol:** 7br; **Bridgeman Art Library** 12bl; **Dreamstime:** Patrick Lamont 22tl; **Getty Images:** MPI 13; **Library of Congress:** 18r, 21r, 26r, 27; **Shutterstock:** 16b, 23br, Jorg Hackermann 6b, Deborah McCague 21b, Rudy Umans 22br; **Thinkstock:** Stephan Barmotov 11br,
Daniel Carevic 11cl, Dorling Kindersley RF 5t, 23l, istockphoto 4, 7bl, 12r, 17c, Photos.com 14; **Topfoto:** British Library Board 14-15c, The Granger Collection 16t, 20, 25t, 25b, 26bl, 28.

All other photos, artwork and maps, **Brown Bear Books Ltd**.

Brown Bear Books has made every attempt to contact the copyright holder. If you have any information please contact licensing@brownbearbooks.co.uk

Library and Archives Canada Cataloguing in Publication

Stuckey, Rachel, author
    Explore with Hernando de Soto / Rachel Stuckey.

(Travel with the great explorers)
Includes index.
Issued in print and electronic formats.
ISBN 978-0-7787-2849-8 (hardback).--ISBN 978-0-7787-2853-5 (paperback).--ISBN 978-1-4271-7728-5 (html)

    1. Soto, Hernando de, approximately 1500-1542--Juvenile literature. 2. Explorers--America--Biography--Juvenile literature. 3. Explorers--Spain--Biography--Juvenile literature. 4. America--Discovery and exploration--Spanish--Juvenile literature. 5. Southern States--Discovery and exploration--Spanish--Juvenile literature. I. Title. I. Series: Travel with the great explorers

E125.S7S88 2016   j910.92   C2016-903345-7
                                        C2016-903346-5

Library of Congress Cataloging-in-Publication Data

Names: Stuckey, Rachel, author.
Title: Explore with Hernando de Soto / Rachel Stuckey.
Description: New York : Crabtree Publishing Company, [2016] | Series: Travel with the great explorers | Includes index.
Identifiers: LCCN 2016023867 (print) | LCCN 2016024183 (ebook) | ISBN 9780778728498 (reinforced library binding) | ISBN 9780778728535 (pbk.) | ISBN 9781427177285 (electronic HTML)
Subjects: LCSH: Soto, Hernando de, approximately 1500-1542--Juvenile literature. | Explorers--America--Biography--Juvenile literature. | Explorers--Spain--Biography--Juvenile literature. | America--Discovery and exploration--Spanish--Juvenile literature. | Southern States--Discovery and exploration--Spanish--Juvenile literature.
Classification: LCC E125.S7 S88 2016 (print) | LCC E125.S7 (ebook) | DDC 910.92 [B] --dc23
LC record available at https://lccn.loc.gov/2016023867

Crabtree Publishing Company

www.crabtreebooks.com   1-800-387-7650

Printed in Canada/072016/EF20160630

Published in Canada
Crabtree Publishing
616 Welland Ave.
St. Catharines, ON
L2M 5V6

Published in the United States
Crabtree Publishing
PMB 59051
350 Fifth Avenue, 59th Floor
New York, New York 10118

Published in the United Kingdom
Crabtree Publishing
Maritime House
Basin Road North, Hove
BN41 1WR

Published in Australia
Crabtree Publishing
3 Charles Street
Coburg North
VIC, 3058

CONTENTS

Meet the Boss

In the early 1500s, the Spaniard Hernando de Soto led the first European expedition into the southeastern United States. De Soto and his men were the first Europeans to cross the Mississippi River.

Did you know?

De Soto was not the first Spanish explorer in Florida. In 1527, Pánfilo de Narváez led an expedition there—and disappeared. Eight years later, just four survivors of the expedition reached Mexico.

POOR LIFE IN SPAIN

+ Noble but poor

+ Young man seeks fortune abroad

Hernando de Soto was born around 1500 in Extremadura, Spain. He came from a **noble** but poor family. Another noble, Pedro Arias Dávila, paid for de Soto to go to university, but opportunities were still limited for the young man in Spain. He wanted to seek fame and fortune in Spain's empire in the Americas. In 1514, when Dávila was named the first governor of Spain's new colony in Panama, de Soto sailed with him to America.

IN THE NAME OF SPAIN

★ Exploring Central America...

In Panama, de Soto became captain of a **cavalry** troop that explored the rain forest (above). In the following years, he served with the Spanish conquerors in Nicaragua and explored Honduras. He became one of the most experienced and powerful **conquistadors**. Just 10 years after arriving in the "New World," he had earned his own **encomienda**, or estate, and a position in the government.

INTO PERU

+ Overthrowing the Inca

+ Conquering new lands

In 1532, de Soto served as a captain on the expedition of Francisco Pizarro to the Inca **Empire** of Peru. The Inca were fighting a civil war, so the Spanish took advantage of their distraction to capture and overthrow the new emperor, Atahualpa. Pizarro and his men shared the gold and silver from the Inca treasury. Pizarro and his captains became very wealthy.

Atahualpa

De Soto became friendly with Atahualpa during his captivity and taught him to play chess. The Inca paid a huge **ransom** in gold for their emperor (above), but the Spaniards killed him anyway.

ORDERED TO FLORIDA

☛ De Soto strikes it rich

☛ Takes control of Cuba

After the conquest of Peru, de Soto (left) returned to Spain. The king made him the governor of Cuba in return for his service. He also ordered de Soto to explore and **colonize** La Florida—the name for Spain's territory in North America, which was a far larger area than what Florida is today. The king and de Soto hoped that La Florida would prove as wealthy as the Inca Empire.

Where Are We Heading?

No one knows de Soto's exact route, but we know he traveled through Florida, Georgia, the Carolinas, Tennessee, Alabama, Mississippi, and Arkansas.

COMING ASHORE

- A natural bay
- Landing in Florida

On May 25, 1539, de Soto's expedition landed in a natural bay on the west coast of Florida. Historians think they came ashore near the mouth of the Manatee River at the southern tip of Tampa Bay (right).

NORTH AMERICA

Florida

Tampa Bay

Manatee River

TRAVEL UPDATE

Keep your feet dry!

★ If you're heading into Florida, be prepared for difficult terrain—and avoid it where possible. As de Soto and his men marched north, they came to the Green Swamp. The swamp, which lies between Tampa and Orlando, is full of obstacles such as **cypress domes** and waters full of alligators. It was so large the expedition had to turn west to travel around its edge.

LIVING IN ANHAICA

+ Overthrowing the Apalachee...

+ ...and seizing their homes

In October 1539, the expedition reached Anhaica, the main town of the Apalachee people in what is now Tallahassee. The Spaniards took over the town, which consisted of 250 buildings, and forced the Apalachee people to move out. In1988, archaeologists found the ruins of Anhaica, as well as evidence that the Spaniards had spent the winter there.

FIRST ACROSS THE MISSISSIPPI

★ Native peoples patrol the river

★ Spaniards sneak across at night

In May 1541, the expedition reached the eastern bank of the Mississippi River, just south of what is now Memphis, Tennessee. Armed warriors in canoes patrolled the river to stop the Spaniards reaching the west bank. De Soto's men built boats and crossed the river at night to avoid an attack. They were the first Europeans to cross the Mississippi River.

NO WEAPONS ALLOWED

☞ Hot springs are neutral territory

☞ Enjoyed by everyone

After crossing the Mississippi, de Soto visited what is now Hot Springs, Arkansas. Several different Native tribes used the **thermal springs**, which they called the Valley of the Vapors. The springs were **neutral** territory, which meant all the tribes laid down their weapons so everyone could enjoy the waters in peace.

> We seek not war with anyone, but our wish is to cultivate peace and friendship. We are in search of a distant province, and all we ask is food during our journey."
> *Hernando de Soto greets warriors in Apalachee.*

DE SOTO'S JOURNEY THROUGH THE SOUTH

Hernando de Soto and his men were the first Europeans to travel throughout what is now the southern United States. After de Soto's death, Luis de Moscoso Alvarado took charge of leading the expedition home.

NORTH AMERICA

Tula

Cayas

Pacah

Casqui

Mississippi River

Texas

Caddo River

At the Caddo River in Arkansas, de Soto and his men clashed with the Tula in spring 1542. The Tula were skilled warriors. They were able to drive away the Spaniards, who returned to the Mississippi River.

Texas

After de Soto's death, Luis de Moscoso Alvarado led the survivors of the expedition into Texas, seeking a way to Mexico. The harsh landscape eventually forced them to turn back to the Mississippi River.

N
NW
NE
W
E
SW
SE
S

Key

→ De Soto's expedition, 1539–1542

→ Moscoso's expedition into Texas, 1542–1543

→ Moscoso's route to Mexico, 1543

Escape Route

Moscoso and his men built boats to float down the Mississippi. They were attacked by Native peoples all the way. The Spaniards then sailed along the Gulf coast and eventually reached Mexico.

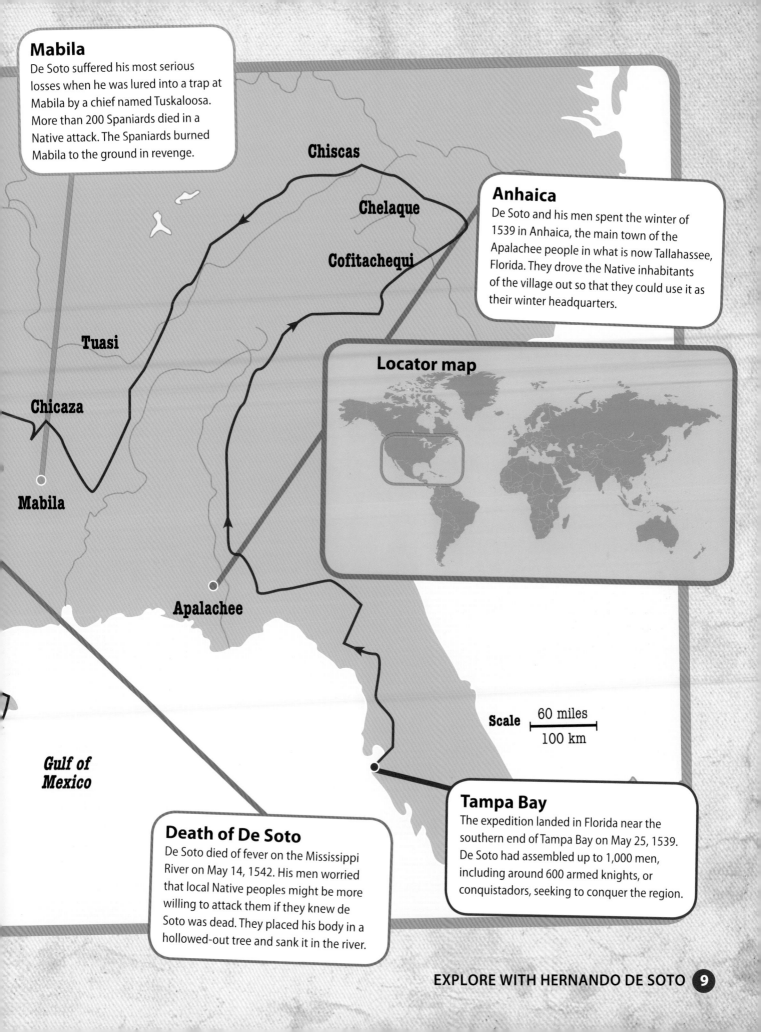

Mabila

De Soto suffered his most serious losses when he was lured into a trap at Mabila by a chief named Tuskaloosa. More than 200 Spaniards died in a Native attack. The Spaniards burned Mabila to the ground in revenge.

Chiscas

Chelaque

Anhaica

De Soto and his men spent the winter of 1539 in Anhaica, the main town of the Apalachee people in what is now Tallahassee, Florida. They drove the Native inhabitants of the village out so that they could use it as their winter headquarters.

Cofitachequi

Tuasi

Locator map

Chicaza

Mabila

Apalachee

Scale 60 miles / 100 km

Gulf of Mexico

Death of De Soto

De Soto died of fever on the Mississippi River on May 14, 1542. His men worried that local Native peoples might be more willing to attack them if they knew de Soto was dead. They placed his body in a hollowed-out tree and sank it in the river.

Tampa Bay

The expedition landed in Florida near the southern end of Tampa Bay on May 25, 1539. De Soto had assembled up to 1,000 men, including around 600 armed knights, or conquistadors, seeking to conquer the region.

Meet the Crew

De Soto's expedition had up to 1,000 men, including priests, engineers, carpenters, and slaves from Africa and the Caribbean. They also enslaved many Native peoples along the way.

HUNGRY FOR CONQUEST

+ Searching for riches...

+ ...and claiming an empire

In the early 1500s, many Spanish men became conquistadors. De Soto was one of many who headed to the Americas in order to search for riches, claim land for Spain, and **convert** Native peoples to Christianity. De Soto's expedition included 600 conquistadors from Spain, Portugal, and North Africa.

FREEING A CAPTIVE

★ **Juan Ortiz held for nine years**

★ **Becomes expedition interpreter**

Almost as soon as de Soto landed in Tampa Bay, he heard stories of another Spaniard in a nearby village! While on an earlier Spanish expedition in 1528, Juan Ortiz had been captured by a Native group. He eventually escaped and lived with another tribe for nine years. De Soto attacked Ortiz's tribe, but stopped when Ortiz called out in Spanish. Ortiz became de Soto's **interpreter**.

LEFT IN CHARGE

☞ **De Soto marries his sweetheart...**

☞ **...She governs Cuba**

During the 1514 voyage in which de Soto sailed to the New World, he fell in love with Isabel de Bobadilla, daughter of Pedro Arias Dávila. They finally married after de Soto made his fortune in Peru in 1534. Isabel governed Cuba while De Soto was away on his expedition. She was the first woman governor of Cuba and the only woman to hold high office in New Spain.

Statue

There is a statue on top of a tower in Havana, Cuba, of a woman looking out to sea (left). Called La Giradilla, it represents Isabel, watching for de Soto's return. Isabel died a year after learning of de Soto's death.

COMMANDER IN THE FIELD

+ Demoted by de Soto

Luis de Moscoso Alvarado was the *maestro de campo*, or field commander of the expedition. After a conflict with the Chicaza people, de Soto took away Moscoso's authority. But when de Soto became ill (right) he chose Moscoso to be the new expedition leader. Moscoso later served as the **viceroy** of New Spain. He died in Peru in 1551.

My Explorer Journal

★ **Historians say that the account of the expedition by El Inca (see below) is more like fiction than a historical record. What sort of things would you look for to decide whether a piece of writing can be considered fact or fiction?**

TELLING THE STORY

★ **Reports of the expedition**

There are three first-hand accounts of the expedition. De Soto's secretary Rodrigo Rangel kept a detailed diary. Luys Hernandez de Biedma wrote a short official report for the king of Spain in 1544. A Portuguese conquistador also wrote an account. In 1605, a Peruvian writer known as El Inca wrote an account of the trip based on talking to survivors. However, historians say that his account is not very reliable.

Check Out the Ride

The expedition arrived in Florida by ship. As de Soto led some explorers inland, either on horseback or on foot, others sailed back to Cuba for supplies before meeting the expedition farther north.

SAILING THE SEAS

+ Ships carry men and supplies

+ Cutting-edge designs

At the time of de Soto's expedition, European shipbuilders had developed different vessels for ocean sailing. Caravels (right) were small, sturdy ships designed by the Portuguese. Their triangular **lateen** sails helped make them fast and **maneuverable**. Caravels were used to cross open oceans. **Brigantines** had two masts with square sails. They were better suited for sailing along the coast.

TRAVEL UPDATE

A question of horsepower!

★ For travelers with more than a few horses, remember that you'll need food for the animals. The Spaniards had about 200 horses, which they used for warfare and transportation. Feeding the horses was a challenge. The Native peoples did not keep any farm animals, so they had none of the hay or other food the horses needed.

I CAN'T SEE MY FEET!

★ **Wading through the swamps**

★ **Keep your balance!**

The dark waters of the Florida swamps were a challenge for foot soldiers and horses alike. The expedition sometimes waded through dark water up to their waists. It was impossible to see the bottom of the swamp, which was covered with tree roots and other obstacles, so it was easy to trip. Progress was slow—and anyone who dropped behind might be attacked by Native warriors angry that the Spaniards were in their territory.

Local Guides

De Soto forced local people to work as guides. These captives acted as translators with people from neighboring territories. Some of these guides led the Spaniards into traps.

MASTER BUILDER

+ **Italian expertise...**

+ **...overcomes obstacles**

In Cuba, De Soto forced an Italian **shipwright** named Maestro Francisco to join the expedition. Francisco directed workers to build bridges and rig ropes to help the expedition cross the swamps and rivers they encountered. The shipwright also built canoes and rafts as they were needed to cross wider rivers.

THE THIRTY LANCERS

☛ **Horsemen retrace their steps**

☛ **Guide ships up the coasts**

When the expedition stopped for the winter in Anhaica, which is now Tallahassee, de Soto sent a group of horsemen back to meet the supply ships returning from Cuba. El Inca's **chronicle** calls these horsemen the Thirty Lancers. They rode for 11 days through the territory of hostile Native peoples to meet the ships. The men and their horses then sailed up to Apalachee Bay to meet up with de Soto.

Did you know?

The Thirty Lancers could not take all their armor on the ships. They left it behind, giving it to a friendly local chief.

Solve It With Science

Even though the Spaniards' guns were not accurate, they were more powerful than Native axes, clubs, and spikes. Native bows and arrows, however, were very effective weapons in the swamps and forests.

The Spanish made excellent armor and weapons from iron and steel. They also milled lumber and built things with metal tools and nails.

GUNPOWDER WEAPONS

☞ Guns are little use...

☞ ...but still terrify the enemy

De Soto's expedition took one small cannon and several guns called **arquebuses** (right). An arquebus was an early version of the rifle. It used gunpowder to fire metal balls as shot. The gun took a long time to load and was not very accurate or powerful. But an arquebus was still frightening to people in the New World who had never seen or used gunpowder before.

SHIPBUILDING

★ From horse tack...

★ ...to ships

At the end of the expedition, the survivors melted down the iron from their horse **tack** and anything else they could find to make nails. They used the nails to build ships to sail down the Mississippi River and along the coast of Mexico to the Panuco River.

UNDER COVER

- Armor protects conquistadors
- But it's too heavy to wear!

The Spaniards wore armor made of iron plates (right). The armor was heavy, however, and restricted their movement. Many men abandoned it for thick cloth armor or chain mail, which was made by joining together tiny metal rings. Chain mail was flexible and offered protection from arrows and spears. Quilted cloth suits offered protection against most wooden weapons, and were lighter and more comfortable to wear than chain mail.

SCIENCE OF ARROWS

+ Arrowheads designed to kill

+ Horses and men fall victim

My Explorer Journal

★ Imagine what it might be like to be traveling through a wet, dark swamp where hostile warriors might be hiding with bows and arrows. How would you keep your spirits up?

The Spanish were impressed by the Native peoples' bows and arrows (above). Using horn, bone, reeds, branches, and feathers, peoples of the Southeast made accurate and deadly arrows. Their archers could shoot arrows faster and farther than European crossbows. And unlike the Spaniards' guns, bows and arrows were silent.

Hanging at Home

De Soto and his men visited many Native villages in Florida. If the Native peoples did not offer them food or places to stay, the Spaniards often simply took them.

Did you know?

To honor their bravery, de Soto invited chiefs and warriors to feasts. But many Native peoples resented the Spanish who had killed their people. A chief named Vitachuco even attacked de Soto during a feast.

LIFE IN THE VILLAGES

☛ Seizing homes...

☛ ...and stealing supplies

The expedition regularly threw Native peoples out of their homes so they could use their village as a base. Most Native houses were constructed from wood and mud, as well as woven mats, bark, or even plaster. There were also storehouses for corn and other crops, which the explorers raided. Many villages were surrounded by **palisades**, but they did not stop the Spaniards. The conquistadors attacked and took whatever supplies they needed.

A VERSATILE CROP

★ Native farmers grow corn...

★ ...and the invaders steal it

Corn was a common crop throughout the Americas, but it was a new food to the Europeans. The expedition often raided village corn supplies, leaving the villagers to starve through the winter. According to the records of the expedition, Native peoples taught de Soto's men how to make corn tortillas.

WHAT'S FOR DINNER?

+ A range of foods

+ Treats for every taste

The Spaniards raided Native crops of squash, beans, and **persimmons** (below). They fished in the rivers and hunted game in the forests. They also learned to gather edible plants from the swamps and forests, such as roots, chestnuts, onions, berries, and hickory nuts. The Spaniards also described eating honey, and making tea from **sassafras**.

KEEPING WARM!

Although Florida was often hot and humid, the temperature could fall steeply, especially at night. Many Spaniards wove blankets from long grasses. They kept off the ground by lying on half of the blanket and covering themselves with the other half. As their clothes wore out, they patched them with woven grass or bark. By the end of the expedition, men were making their own clothes from animal skins.

TOUGH LIFE

★ Living in camp

★ Struggling for food

When they did not stay in Native villages, the expedition set up camps in forests and fields (left). The camps were not very pleasant places to live. The Spaniards were often short of food, and they also lacked equipment such as blankets to make them comfortable. Some men cleared a space to build rough shelters to sleep in, while others set out to try to find food to feed the expedition's horses.

Meeting and Greeting

The Spaniards often named a Native village after its most powerful leader. The names the Native peoples themselves used for many of their villages are now lost to history.

TAKING A STAND

- ☛ **Florida chief attacks de Soto**
- ☛ **Pays with his life**

Vitachuco, a chief in central Florida, made an angry speech telling the Spaniards to leave his people alone (right). De Soto put him under house arrest. One night, Vitachuco tried to kill de Soto at a feast. During the fighting that followed, the chief was killed.

FIGHTING BACK

- ★ **Timuca peoples kill Spaniards...**
- ★ **... but are still defeated**

The Timuca peoples of northern Florida (left) had met Spaniards before de Soto arrived. They had met Spanish explorers in 1513 and 1528. Chief Acuera and his people fought back against de Soto's men when the Spaniards seized food and took **hostages**. They did not stop de Soto, but they did kill 14 conquistadors.

RECLAIMING THE CITY

+ Farmers and traders...

+ ... with stories of gold

The Apalachee were farmers who traded with Native peoples to the north for copper items. When other tribes told de Soto about this copper, the Spaniards thought it was gold. They seized the Apalachee capital, Anhaica. The Apalachee fought back with raiding parties and ambushes. Their arrows could penetrate Spanish soldiers' chain mail. The Native warriors also targeted the conquistadors' horses.

My Explorer Journal

★ **Some Native peoples cooperated with de Soto to prevent trouble, while some tried to drive the Spaniards away. If you were a Native person at that time, do you think you would have cooperated or fought back? Give reasons for your choices.**

> Their canoes, which were neatly made and of great size, and with their awnings, colored feathers, and waving standards, appeared like a fleet of galleys." *The Portuguese chronicler describes Aquixo's canoes.*

BLOCKING THE WAY

☛ **Canoes on the Mississippi**

☛ **Driven away by Spaniards**

A chief named Aquixo tried to stop the Spaniards from crossing the Mississippi. He and his warriors sailed down the river in a fleet of hundreds of canoes (left). Although he sent de Soto presents of fruit, he refused to land to greet the Spaniards. He may have feared being taken captive. The Spaniards drove off the canoes with their guns and crossbows. They later crossed the river in four boats under cover of night.

LADY OF COFITACHEQUI

★ **Powerful beauty greets De Soto...**

★ **... and is taken hostage**

The chiefs of Cofitachequi ruled their part of what is now South Carolina for 400 years. In 1540, the **chieftain** of Cofitachequi was a woman. She was rowed across a river in a decorated canoe to meet de Soto. The Spaniards did not record her name, but they said that she was beautiful and wise. Nevertheless, such qualities did not stop the Spaniards from taking her hostage.

The Mississippian Peoples

De Soto and his men were probably the only Europeans to meet the Mississippian peoples. Their way of life was in decline when the Spaniards arrived.

Did you know?

When the Spaniards arrived in central Georgia, the chief of the Ichisi people sent a messenger to ask three questions: "Who are you?" "What do you want?" and "Where are you going?"

THE BIGGEST BATTLE

★ **Tuskaloosa is a strong leader**

★ **Attacks the Spaniards at Mabila**

Tuskaloosa was a powerful leader in what is now Alabama. The Spaniards took him hostage and occupied his village, Mabila. Tuskaloosa organized a successful attack against the conquistadors in Mabila (right). The Spanish eventually won, but they suffered many losses.

CHICAZA

☛ **Nighttime attack**

As they passed through Alabama, the expedition stayed in a Chicaza village. After some minor arguments, the Chicaza turned against the Spaniards. They launched a nighttime attack that chased the Spanish away. The Chicaza are one of the few tribes whose Native name survived the years following de Soto's visit. In English, they were called the Chickasaw.

> "We beg you to pray to your God to bring us rain, for our fields are parched from lack of water!" *Chief Casqui speaks to de Soto, according to Spanish accounts.*

NEIGHBORLY DISPUTES

★ Spaniards asked to take sides

★ De Soto refuses

De Soto and his men left destruction wherever they went. But some Mississippian peoples tried to use the arrival of the Spaniards to their advantage. In eastern Arkansas, the Casqui accompanied the expedition to attack their enemies, the Pacaha. They seized bones from the Pacaha temples as trophies. De Soto eventually arranged a peace between the warring peoples.

RAISING A CROSS

+ Preaching Christianity

The Casqui lived in fortified villages in eastern Arkansas. They seemed to be open to the teachings of the priests who accompanied the Spaniards. A huge tree was cut down and Maestro Francisco used it to construct a huge cross that was set up on a hill overlooking the village (right). The priests preached sermons to the Casqui. It may be that the people were eager to try any kind of worship they hoped might end the drought they were suffering from.

A FADING CULTURE

☛ Mississippians build large mounds

☛ Store the bones of the dead

The Mississippian peoples built large mounds for temples and **ossuaries**, where they kept the bones of their ancestors. A chieftain ruled over several villages within a territory. Very few Mississippian cultures survived the next century, so most of our knowledge of them comes from archaeology and the records of the de Soto expedition.

I Love Nature

The de Soto chroniclers describe many different types of animals, such as deer and mountain lions, as well as useful plants such as sassafras.

Gators!

Later French explorers claimed the alligators of Florida were bigger than the crocodiles of the Nile in Egypt. But the chroniclers with de Soto never even mention seeing alligators in Florida!

WILD HOGS

- First pigs in the Americas
- Their descendants still live

There were no pigs in the Americas before the Spanish arrived. De Soto brought an unknown number of pigs to Florida—some sources say there were over 200 pigs at the start. By the time he died, de Soto himself owned 700 pigs. Along the way, pigs were eaten or traded, and some escaped into the wilderness. Today's wild hogs or razorbacks of the Southeastern United States and Texas are descendants of de Soto's pigs.

CREATURES OF THE WETLANDS

+ Swamps harbor many creatures

The expedition had to cross many swamps in Florida. The swamps had thick marshlands and cypress domes. Many animals live in the swamplands, including songbirds, wading birds, wild turkeys, black bears, and alligators (right). The Spaniards must have seen alligators in the swamps—but records of the expedition do not even mention these now-famous giant reptiles.

GIANT FISH

- Fish with whiskers
- Good for food

West of the Mississippi, de Soto's men saw giant catfish they called *bagres*. These fish had large heads with whiskers at the sides of their mouths. Some of them were huge. The people of Pacaha, a large town on the Arkansas River, used fishing **weirs** to catch them.

My Explorer Journal

★ De Soto's expedition may have come across alligators in the Florida swamps. Using the picture on these pages, and any you may find online, write a description of an alligator for someone who has never seen one.

A WOOLLY OX

+ Chief gives de Soto a gift
+ But what beast is it from?

The American bison or buffalo (left) once lived as far east as the western Carolinas and as far south as northern Florida. But the de Soto chronicles never mention seeing buffalo. A chief did give the Spaniards an animal hide they said was as thin as calf's skin with soft hair. The Europeans thought it came from an ox, but it was probably buffalo hide.

WHITE GOLD

★ Oysters produce pearls
★ As valuable as precious metal

In Georgia, the Spaniards were excited to find pearls. The oysters of the Coosa River produced beautiful pearls the size of hazelnuts. But the Spanish were shocked to learn that Native peoples used heat to open the oysters. That discolored the pearls, which in Europe would make them far less valuable.

Fortune Hunting

Spanish conquistadors had found great wealth in the Aztec Empire in Mexico and the Inca Empire in Peru. De Soto hoped to find more riches in La Florida—but he was disappointed.

WHERE'S THE GOLD?

+ De Soto asks everyone the question...

+ ... but never finds the answer

Finding riches was the main reason the Spaniards explored the Americas. De Soto had made a fortune in the conquest of the Incan Empire. He believed he would find even more gold in La Florida. Wherever he went, he asked Native peoples about gold. He often changed his route to investigate rumors of gold. Although some Native peoples did find gold (right), there were no rich supplies of the metal. De Soto found nothing of value but copper and pearls.

EMPIRE-BUILDING

★ Claiming land for Spain...

★ ... but Spain doesn't want it!

One reason the king and queen of Spain sent de Soto to explore La Florida was to expand the Spanish Empire by setting up colonies. Colonies enabled the Spanish to rule the local population and take **resources** from the land. De Soto discovered, however, that La Florida did not have any resources that Spain wanted or needed. After his expedition, the Spaniards gave up the idea of setting up colonies throughout the South.

A PERFECT CLIMATE!

The Spaniards realized that the warm, humid climate of the South made it ideal for growing crops. Native peoples were skilled farmers (right). There were also wild nuts and berries. De Soto fed his army by hunting, gathering, and stealing food stores from small villages. There was also plenty of wood for building shelters.

Did you know?

De Soto told local Native peoples that he was a child of the Sun and **immortal**. He hoped that might make them too afraid to attack the expedition.

SAVING SOULS

☛ A different sort of profit

☛ Gaining converts to Christianity

Spanish expeditions always included Catholic priests, who often served as translators and held mass for the conquistadors. The priests also tried to convert Native peoples to Christianity. This was supposed to save their souls and make it easier for the Spanish to control them. However, De Soto didn't stay anywhere long enough to convert the peoples of La Florida.

This Isn't What It Said in the Brochure!

De Soto and his men faced many challenges on their march through the new territories. They were often attacked. There were also physical hardships, illness, and food shortages.

LOST IN THE SWAMP

★ **Experienced soldier gives up**

★ **Heads for home**

Vasco Porcallo de Figueroa was an experienced conquistador who helped pay for the expedition. Shortly after he reached Florida, he fell from his horse while trying to capture a local chief in a swamp (right). Porcallo was so discouraged, he decided the whole expedition would be a failure. He quit and returned with his men to Cuba, although they left their supplies behind.

TUSKALOOSA'S TRAP

☛ **Attack at Mabila**

☛ **Thousands killed**

Chief Tuskaloosa led de Soto to his village, Mabila. It was a trap. Hundreds of warriors were hiding in the houses. When the Spaniards arrived, the warriors attacked (left). More than 2,000 Native people were killed. However, while only 200 Spaniards died and 150 were injured, it was the greatest Spanish loss of the expedition. As punishment, they burned the town.

TRAVEL UPDATE

Keep everyone onside!

★ One potential problem on a long expedition is the danger of a **mutiny**. After three years, some of de Soto's soldiers wanted to quit. De Soto threatened to behead anyone who tried to leave. He declared, "Whilst I live, no one shall quit this country until we have conquered and settled it." Instead of heading back to the ships, de Soto led his men farther west.

My Explorer Journal

★ De Soto had to convince his restless men not to give up. If you were leading the expedition, what would you say to try to stop your companions from turning around and heading home?

Why do you desire to return to Spain? Have you left any **hereditary** estates that you wish to enjoy?" *De Soto addresses his restless soldiers.*

Attack!

During most of their journey, the Spaniards encountered Native warriors trying to drive them away. The warriors used guerrilla **tactics**, such as ambushing small groups, attacking at night, or firing arrows from cover.

DEATH OF AN EXPLORER

☛ De Soto falls sick

☛ Leaves few possessions behind

On May 14, 1542, de Soto became ill with fever—probably **malaria**. He died on May 21 near the Mississippi River in Arkansas. He named Luis de Moscoso Alvarado as his replacement. When de Soto died, his personal possessions included four native slaves, three horses, and 700 pigs.

End of the Road

The Spanish government considered de Soto's expedition a complete failure. He had found no gold or riches, established no settlements, and did not make any converts to Christianity.

A SECRET BURIAL

☞ **How can an immortal die?**

☞ **Buried in the Mississippi**

Because de Soto had told local people he was a child of the Sun, they believed he was immortal. The Spaniards were afraid that the Native peoples would find out that de Soto had died, and be more likely to attack them. Moscoso and his men placed de Soto's body in a hollowed-out tree trunk, then sank it in the Mississippi River at night (left).

DEVASTATING CONSEQUENCES

★ **Natives hit by deadly disease**

★ **Whole peoples disappear**

De Soto's expedition was a disaster for the native population of La Florida. De Soto and his men killed thousands of Native people and left others to starve. Epidemics of diseases carried from Europe by the Spaniards reduced the Native population enough to change their society. Villages were abandoned, tribes collapsed, and survivors formed new tribes and cultures. By the time French and British explorers arrived a century later, most of the villages and people described in the de Soto chronicles no longer existed.

★ Imagine that you are a tribal leader meeting European explorers many years after the de Soto expedition. From the information in this book about de Soto's treatment of Native peoples, write a speech explaining why you do not trust the Europeans.

THE MOSCOSO EXPEDITION

+ Spaniards head for Mexico

After de Soto died, Luis de Moscoso Alvarado led the men toward Mexico through Texas. The land was so dry that they turned back. In June 1543, they sailed down the Mississippi to the Gulf of Mexico. They were attacked nearly all the way by Native warriors (above). They sailed along the Texas coast to the Pánuco River. From there, they traveled overland to Mexico City.

No Thanks!

About 300 conquistadors survived the expedition. Some of these survivors believed they had quit the journey too soon—but none of the survivors volunteered to return to La Florida!

TRAVEL UPDATE

Keep track of your...tracks!

★ If you think your journey might be important, keep a record of it! De Soto left no maps, so no one is sure exactly where he traveled. In 1939, the United States De Soto Expedition Commission established an "official" route (left). Today, researchers are still trying to confirm the route using archaeology and accounts of the journey passed on through local stories.

TENNESSEE NORTH

MISSISSIPPI

ALABAMA

GEORGIA

CAROLINA

Course

De Soto's Course

Tampa Bay
1539

GLOSSARY

arquebuses Early long-barreled guns

brigantines Two-masted sailing ships

cavalry Soldiers who fight on horseback

chieftain The leader of a group of people

chronicle An account of historical events

colonize To move into another place and set up settlements

conquistador Spanish adventurers who conquered South America and Mexico

convert To give up one religion for another, or to persuade someone else to do so

cypress domes Dense swamps with many cypress trees that look like domes from far away

empire A large area ruled over by one person

encomienda Land given by the Spanish monarch to settlers in the New World

guerrilla Describes irregular military tactics

hereditary Passed on from one generation to another

hostages People taken captive until a certain condition is fulfilled

immortal Living forever

interpreter A person who translates language as it is spoken

lateen A triangular sail at the front or back of a ship

malaria A fever that is sometimes deadly

maneuverable Can change direction easily

mutiny A rebellion by soldiers against their commanding officers

neutral Not belonging to one group or another

noble Belonging to the aristocracy

ossuaries Places where the bones of dead people are kept

palisades Fences made of wooden stakes

persimmons Fruits resembling a tomato

ransom Money that is demanded for the release of a prisoner

resources Useful natural materials

sassafras A tree with aromatic leaves

shipwright Someone who builds ships

tack Equipment used to ride a horse, such as bridles, stirrups, and saddles

thermal springs Naturally hot springs

viceroy Someone who rules a region on behalf of a king or queen

weirs Stakes set in a river to trap fish

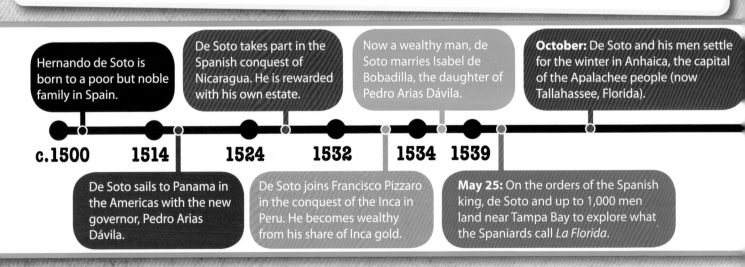

Hernando de Soto is born to a poor but noble family in Spain.

De Soto takes part in the Spanish conquest of Nicaragua. He is rewarded with his own estate.

Now a wealthy man, de Soto marries Isabel de Bobadilla, the daughter of Pedro Arias Dávila.

October: De Soto and his men settle for the winter in Anhaica, the capital of the Apalachee people (now Tallahassee, Florida).

c.1500   1514   1524   1532   1534   1539

De Soto sails to Panama in the Americas with the new governor, Pedro Arias Dávila.

De Soto joins Francisco Pizarro in the conquest of the Inca in Peru. He becomes wealthy from his share of Inca gold.

May 25: On the orders of the Spanish king, de Soto and up to 1,000 men land near Tampa Bay to explore what the Spaniards call *La Florida*.

ON THE WEB

www.history.com/topics/exploration/hernando-de-soto
History.com page on de Soto with videos and links.

www.mrnussbaum.com/desoto/
A student-friendly teaching resource with a biography of de Soto.

www.floridahistory.com/inset44.html
A Florida history site that attempts to reconstruct the route followed by de Soto and his expedition.

www.learnnc.org/lp/editions/nchist-twoworlds/1694
A page from the North Carolina Digital History project about archaeological research into the de Soto expedition.

www.biography.com/people/hernando-de-soto-38469
A biography of de Soto from biography.com.

BOOKS

Goldberg, Jan. *Hernando de Soto: Trailblazer of the American Southeast* (Library of Explorers and Exploration). Rosen Publishing Group, 2003.

Hubbard-Brown, Janet. *Hernando de Soto and His Expeditions Across the Americas* (Explorers of New Lands). Chelsea House Publications, 2005.

Petrie, Kristin. *Hernando de Soto* (Explorers). Checkerboard Library, 2004.

Young, Jeff C. *Hernando de Soto: Spanish Conqueror in the Americas* (Great Explorers of the World). Enslow Publishing Ltd, 2009.

October 18: De Soto loses 200 men in an attack by Chief Tuskaloosa at Mabila in Alabama.

May 8: The expedition arrives on the east bank of the Mississippi River; they cross it a few weeks later.

May 21: After falling sick a week earlier, de Soto dies on the banks of the Mississippi. His body is buried in the river.

September 10: Having traveled along the Gulf coast, the survivors of the expedition reach Spanish territory at the Pánuco River in Mexico.

1540 **1541** **1542** **1543**

December 18: De Soto goes into winter quarters at Chicaza, Mississippi. His men are driven out by a Native attack two months later.

October: De Soto's men clash with the Tula at the Caddo River in Arkansas.

July 2: After failing to reach Mexico across the Texas desert, Luis de Moscoso Alvarado and the other Spaniards sail down the Mississippi River. They are attacked by Native peoples all the way.

INDEX